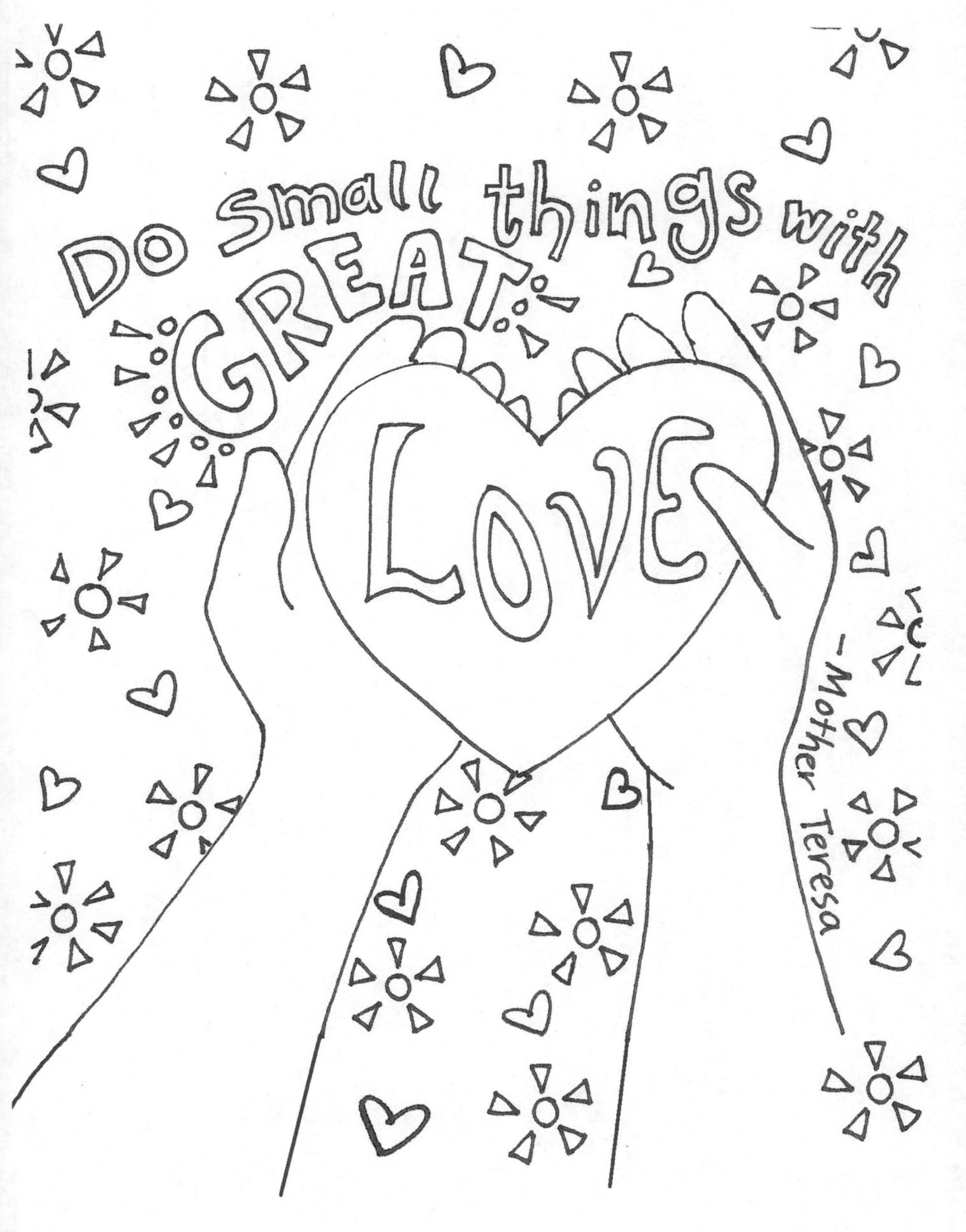

hold hands
not grudges

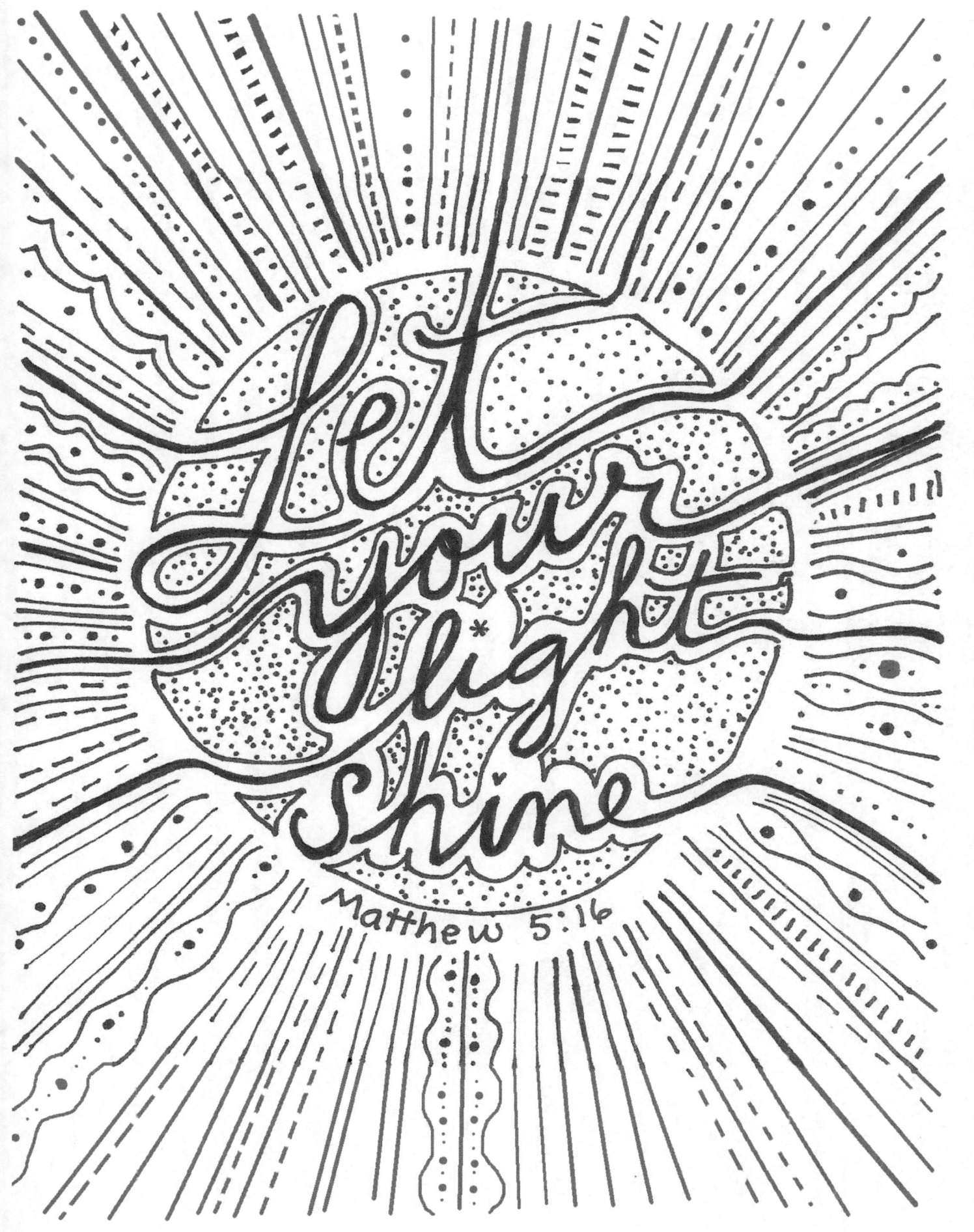

The Purest & most thoughtful minds are those which Love COLOR the most —John Ruskin

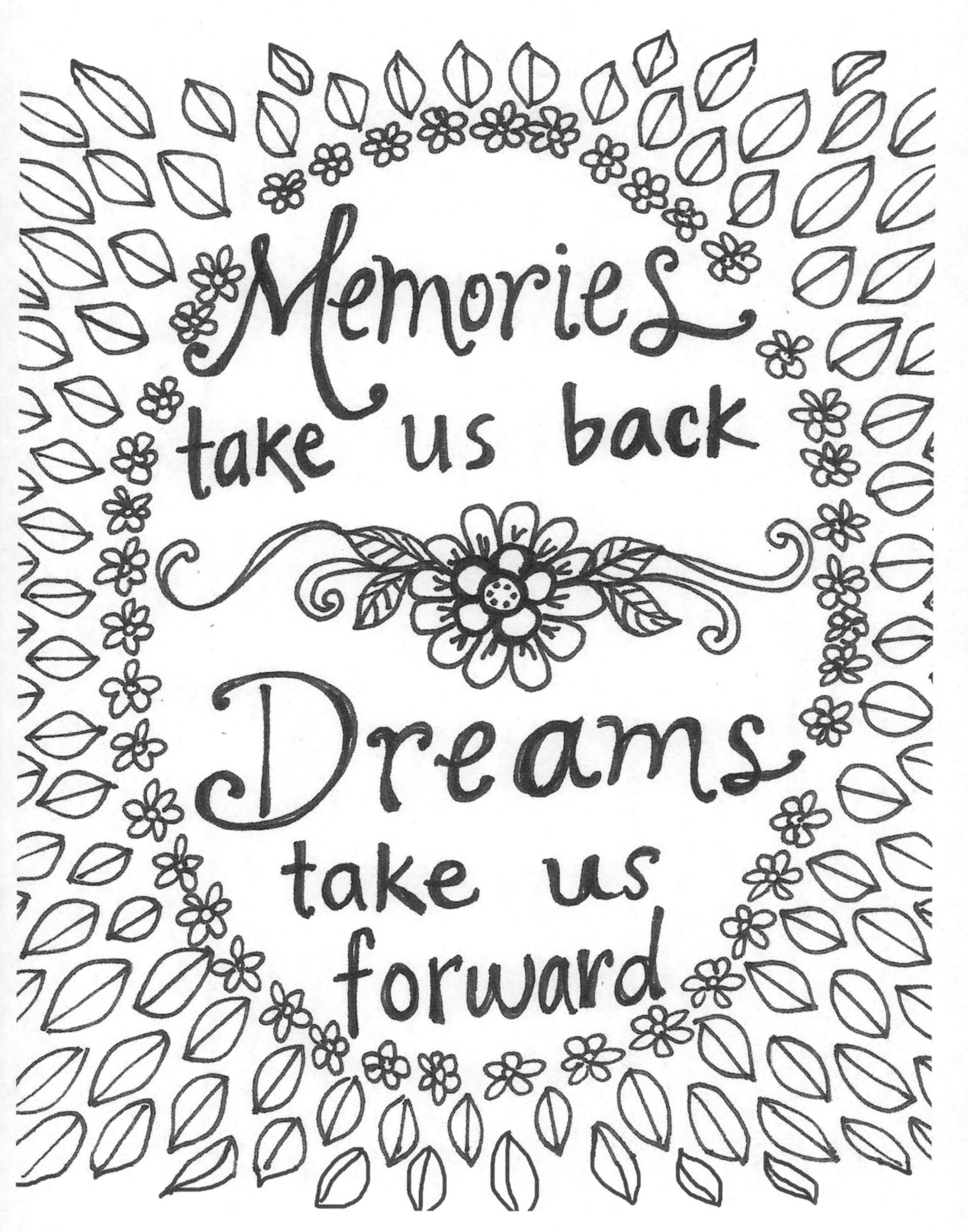

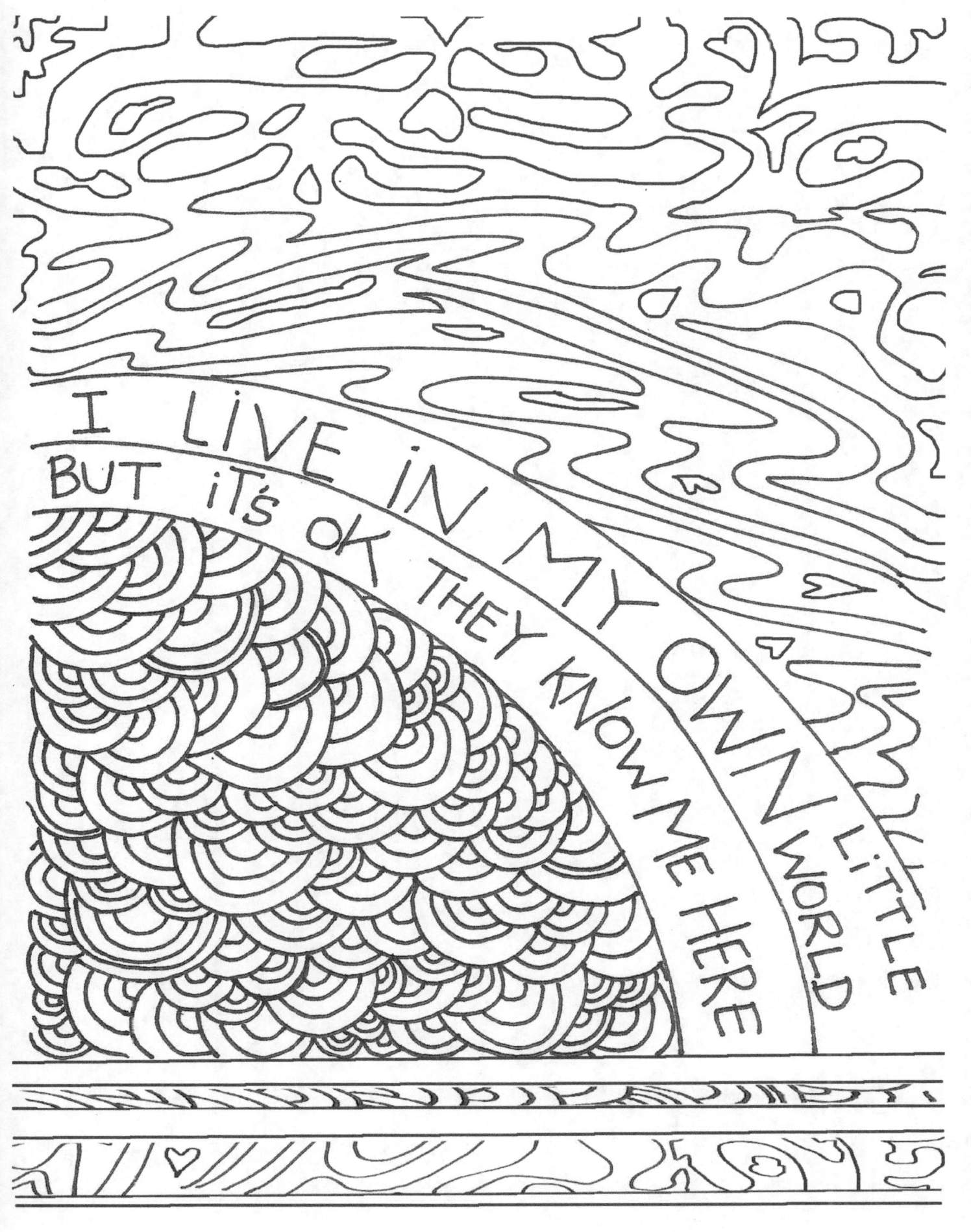

I LIVE iN MY OWN Little WORLD BUT iT's oK THEY KNoW ME HERE

THE TALLEST OAK in the forest was once just a little nut that held it's ground

Christa Valenti

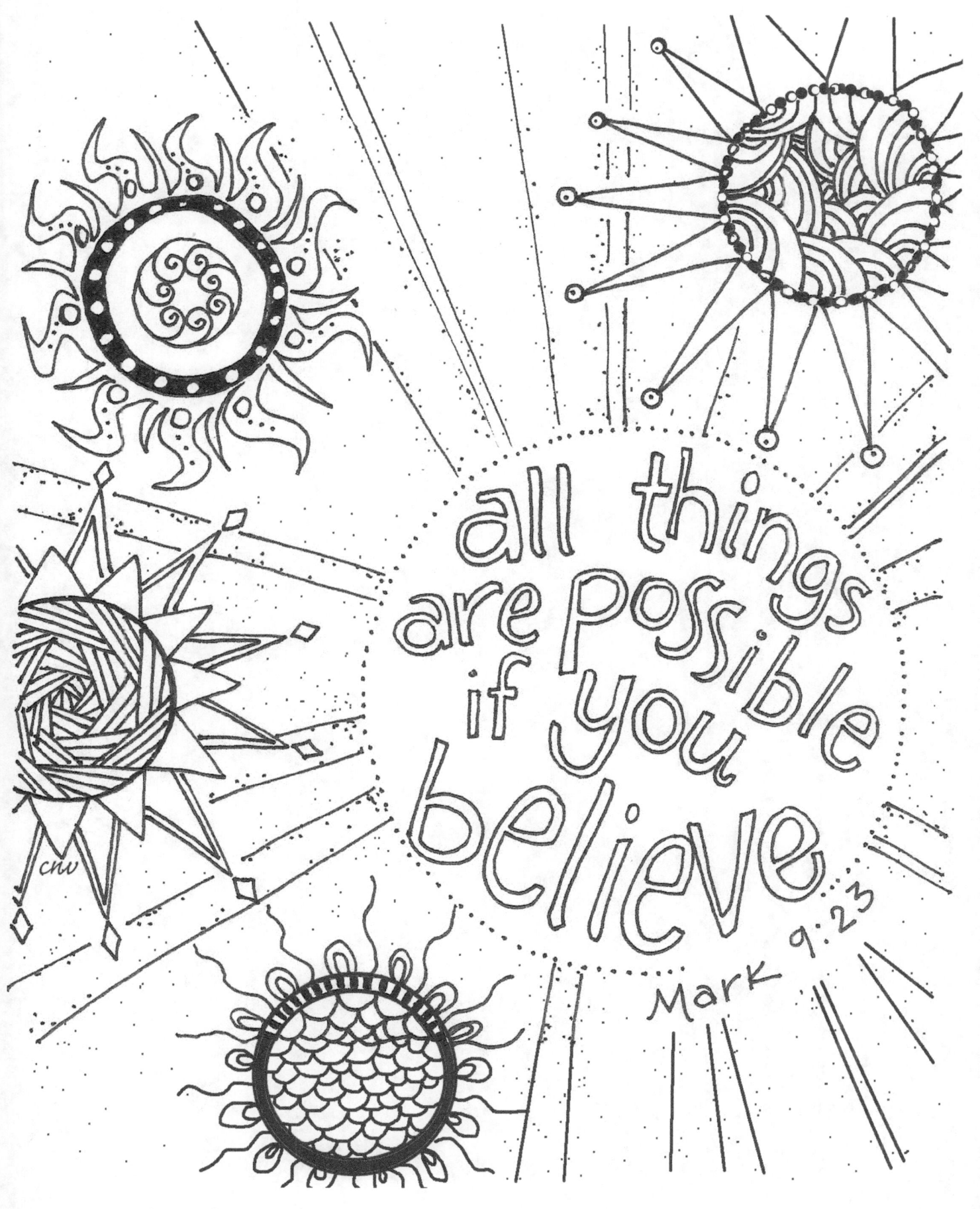

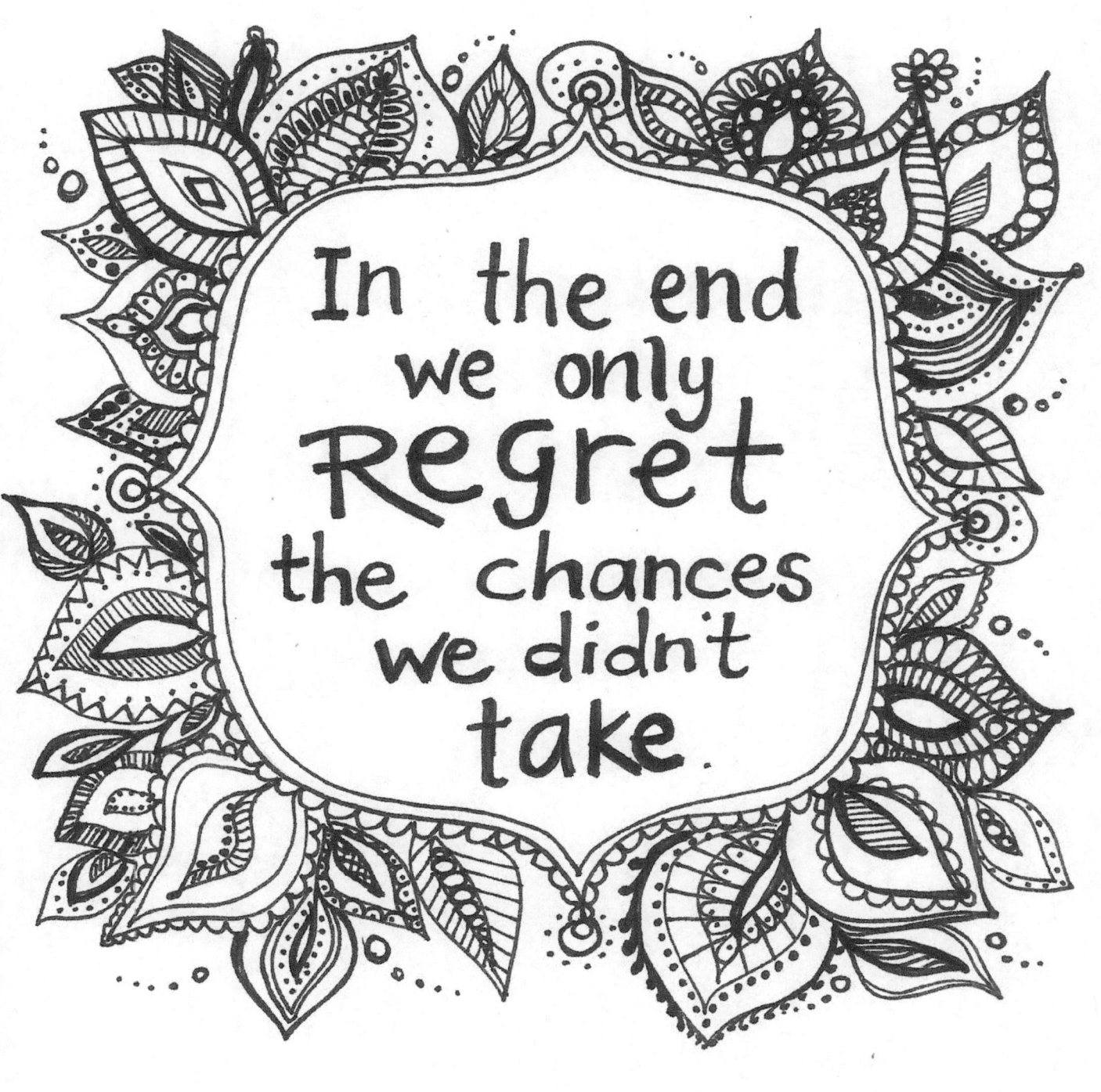

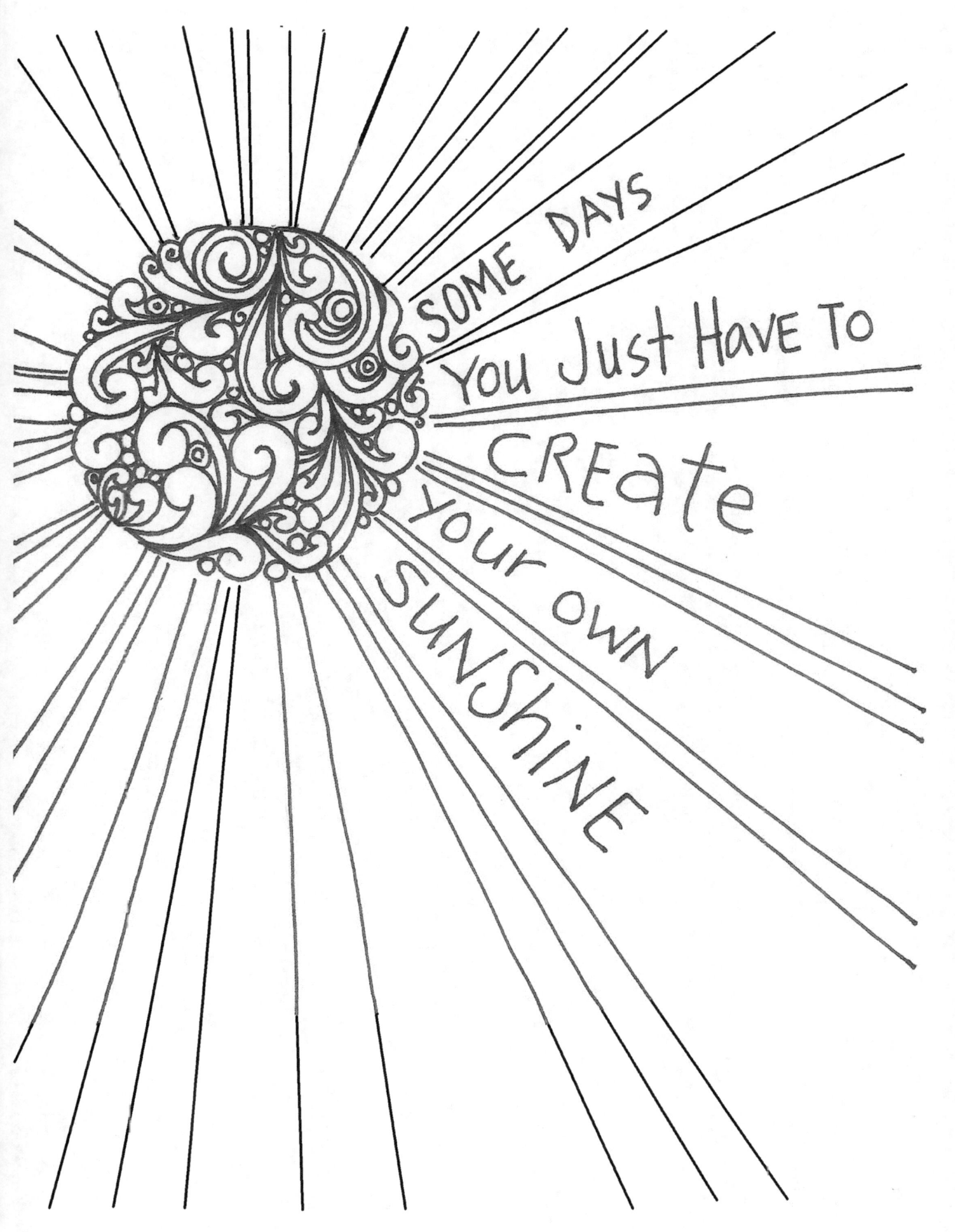

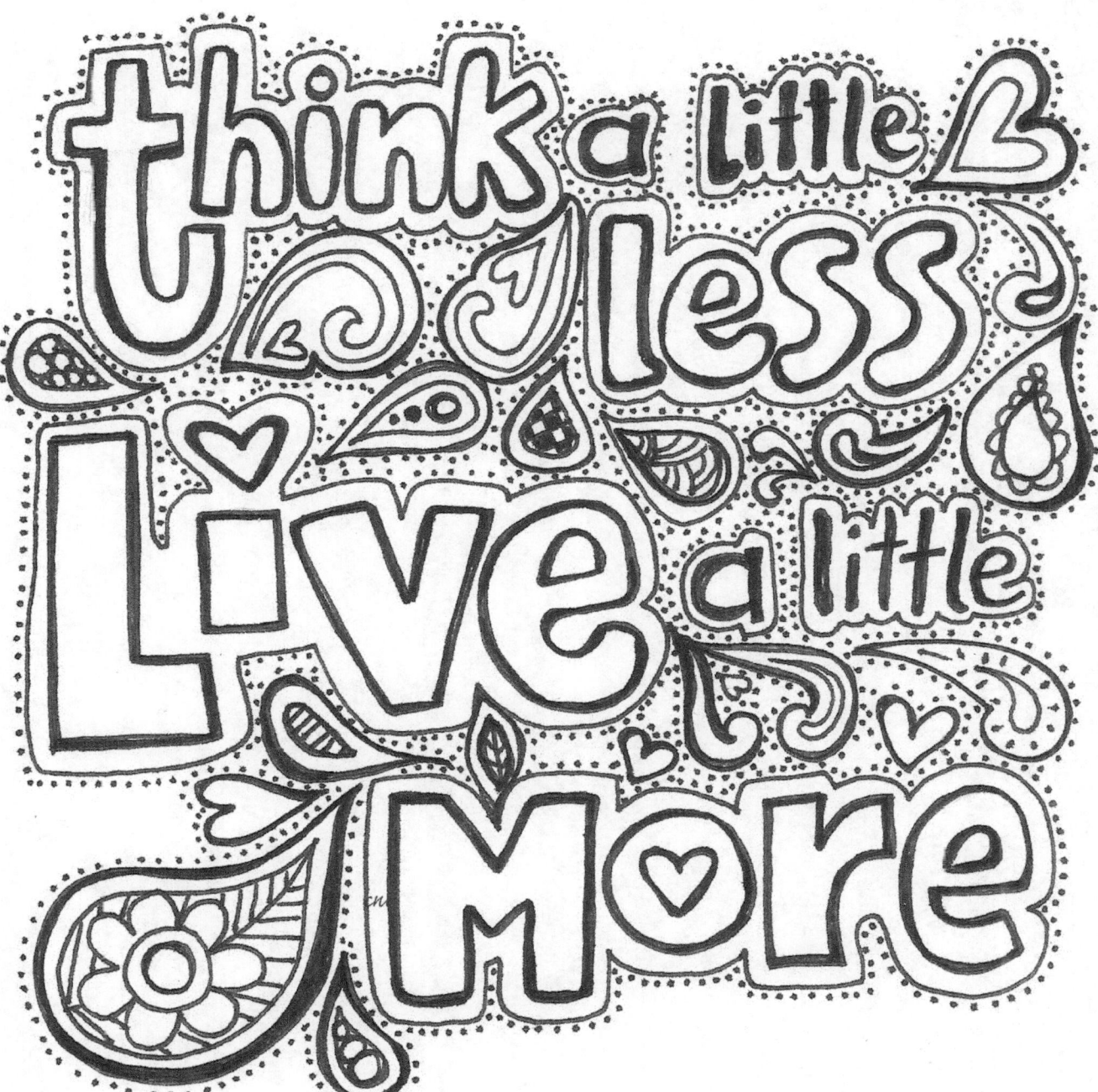

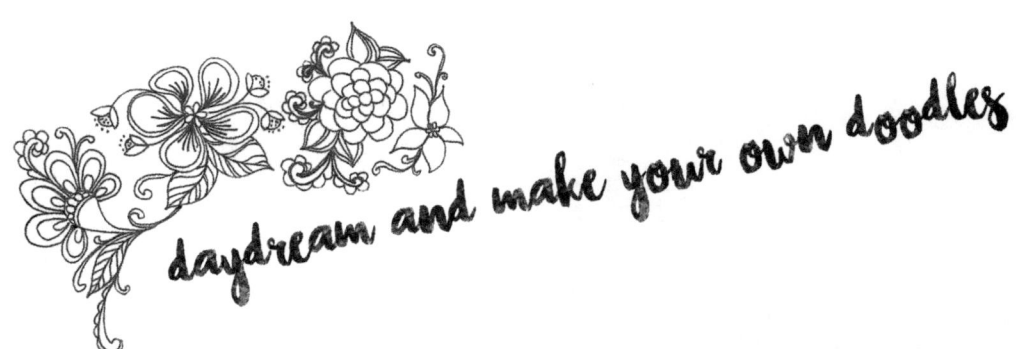

daydream and make your own doodles